I0493311

Table of Contents

Hi There.

For all the people who have no idea how to invest - now you can stop asking me questions.

(Thanks for reading).

- Mike

Who This is For?

Or: Give this to your nephew/niece who just graduated as a last minute gift because you forgot

The Key Points
1. This is where I'll summarize the whole chapter in about five bullet points
2. You need to save
   1. you need to save more than you think
   2. you can spend less
3. Investing is easy
4. Debt is evil

This book is for someone who knows nothing about money (me 5 years ago).

The book is split into three chapters, which have official titles but also have unofficial titles:

1. SAVE MORE MONEY YOU STUPID IDIOT
2. Investing, or "Buy an index fund and shut up"
3. Debt is evil spelled incorrectly

This is for anyone who has just graduated college and is (hopefully) getting their first "adult" job. The kind with a 401(k). What the heck is a 401(k)??? All in good time. The time is now - its a retirement account. Aka the thing you're going to be happy you started saving early for 40 years in the future.

I've had a lot of people ask me some very basic questions about how to invest their money. This is my quick way to help answer them, and anyone else who hasn't asked me but wanted to. Also I don't know a ton of people, so I felt this might be more appropriate.

The truth is I was a financial advisor for a little bit. I left the industry in a hurry because it didn't seem like the people I worked with knew much about what they were talking about. They just wanted to push products on people. That doesn't seem right.

This is a book meant to help people. Its simple and easy to read. And it's really short. I know kids these days (I'm one of them) apparently have short attention spans.

I hope this book can help anyone, and hopefully even be a little interesting. Good luck, I hope to see you in 40 years rich, fat, and in high spirits.

Chapter 1:
The Importance of Saving

Or: STOP SPENDING MONEY ON
EVERYTHING YOU BIG DUMMY

The Key Points
1. **Save as much as possible**
2. **Save even more**
3. **You can spend less, do it you idiot**

Saving Is The Most Important Thing You'll Ever Do

Hi there! Welcome to the first real chapter of the book! I hope you are doing well; I'm doing well. Well, I imagine I'm doing well. As I'm writing this, I'm doing well, so I hope I still am while you're reading this (whenever that is). Hm. I think we're getting off track.

You picked up this book because you wanted to know how to invest. But before we start talking about investing money, it's important to learn that you should be saving money. Almost 26% of adults in America have no savings. The average savings in a bank account is a little over $4,000. The average savings rate, the amount people put into a savings account at a bank is around only 5%! That means for every $100 you are paid, you are likely only to save $5. The savings rate in America has gone down a lot over the years. Just look at this chart:

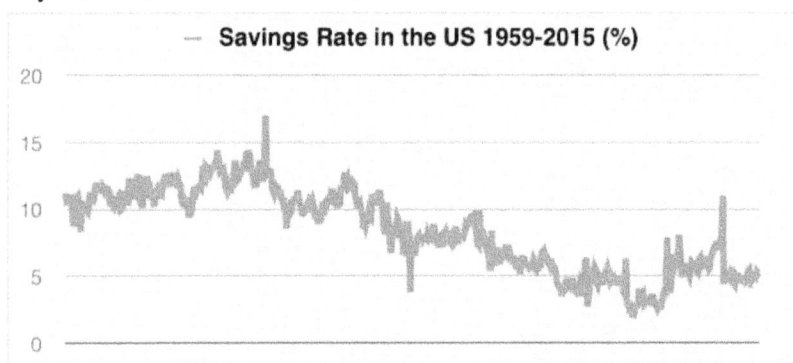

That is not a lot of saving going on. So I'm going to ask you to try and save 10%. Double! Mike that's too much! You can do it, and you should do it. You can, and should, save 10% of your take-home pay.

I know there are a lot of things in your life that have to be paid (essentials like housing). There is also a lot of stuff that you are paying for that doesn't have to be (non-essentials, like that 5th pair of shoes).

The big stuff should get paid: student loans, car payments, insurance, rent. But (if you haven't already bought a car and need one) ask yourself if you need a fantastic car, or more realistically a good car that will get you from point a to point b. I bought a used Honda Civic. It's a good car that will get me to point a to point b, and I intend to drive that thing until it becomes a Flintstones car and I have to move it with my feet through the floor. (That might be a stretch, but you get it).

Next up is housing. I'm going to make this simple - you probably don't need a house. I don't know your living situation, but most people in the 20+ range don't need to own a house. There are too many costs associated with it. The mortgage, plus mortgage insurance. Plus home insurance. Plus upkeep costs. Plus property taxes. The amount most people think about (the mortgage) is just the surface.

If you can rent, and with a roommate, go for it! Splitting the costs is, of course, an excellent way to save. Most apartments to rent don't charge much more for each person, so the cost of renting goes down dramatically with each individual added. But even that might be a bit too costly.

Live with your parents if you can. I know you might want to get out of the house as fast as possible, and you might think your parents think the same thing. But I'm going to bet that they love you very much and would be happy to have you. I'm not saying live there forever. I'm saying that at the beginning of your adult life it's not the end of the world. Living on your own as an adult is a very western idea anyways. My coworkers who have grown up in other countries have their entire household (parents, kids, grandparents) all in one house. It is perfectly acceptable to live with your parents, and I do currently. It's a great way to save money (you should pay them a bit of rent if possible).

Let's look at your saving now. 10%. That's the goal. I think it's very doable, especially if you can cut on your housing costs like I detailed above. Every month, try to remember to move 10% of your paycheck into your savings account. Let's illustrate this with the below chart. Two people make $50,000 a year. Person A saves 5% a year, but he invests very well and makes 10% a year in the stock market. Person B doesn't invest at all but saves 10% of their paycheck a year. How does it play out?

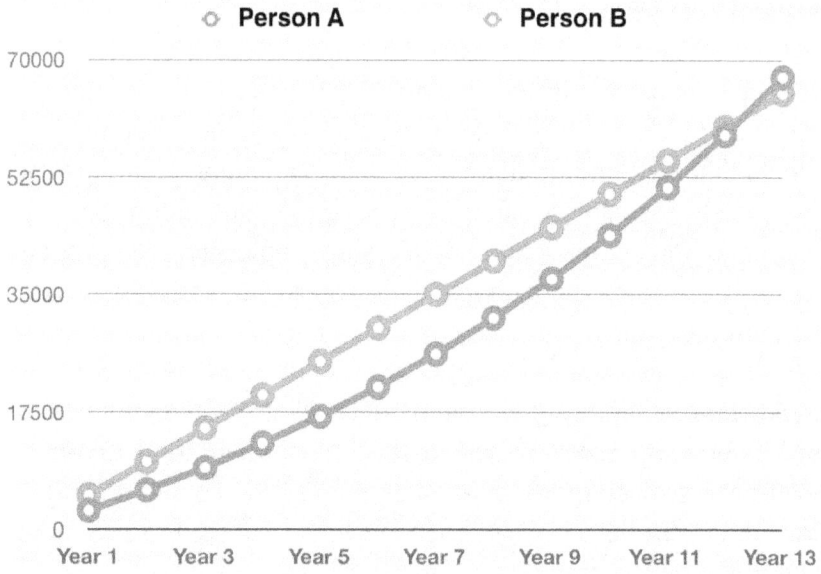

Wow. It takes 13 years of investing just to catch up to the person who simply saved 10% of their paycheck each year. Imagine if any of Person B's savings had been invested, and had gotten even a

2% return each year. The point is simple - saving beats everything else by a long shot.

But how do you make sure you can save that much?

I'm going to ask you to do some work. Tragic, I know. Write down a list of all the things you pay for. Do it for a month. It might highlight that it turns out, little to your knowledge, that you keep spending $100 a weekend at the bar. Or that maybe you don't need to spend $7 every morning on an iced mocha frappe. I'm not saying give up coffee (seriously, trust me, I drink about 7 cups a day. That is not hyperbole). I'm saying maybe make your coffee. Or use the company coffee. Or only get that $7 iced mocha frappe every other day.

When I wrote down all my costs for a month, I realized I was still subscribing to a magazine I never read anymore. I realized that I got a lot of sushi delivered from down the street in a month. I still eat sushi, but not as much, and I try not to get it delivered all the time, which adds up (tips, "minimum delivery amounts" that make me buy extra, etc).

So the two big points here: saving as much as possible as early as possible can be incredibly helpful in the long run, and we probably all pay too much for things we don't need (groundbreaking, I know, but it had to be said).

Emergency Savings

The Key Points
1. **Save 3-6 months worth of expenses**
2. **Lots of bad things happen that we don't plan for**
    1. **we can plan to be able to deal with bad things when they do happen, however**

Be Smart

Being smart about spending your money is as important as investing what you have left. Saving money so you can cover your expected costs (and more likely the expected costs of the fun things that you want to do) is important. But it is also important to drive home one more point - the need to save for what you can't expect.

In a study by Prudential, people were asked to pin on a board significant events from the past five years on a timeline. Yellow magnets represented the good memories, while blue magnets represented the bad memories. Guess what happened at the end? There was a pretty even mix of yellow and blue, good and bad. There were car accidents, deaths, births, first dates, you name it.

Next people were asked to look into the future and predict good and bad events. Yellow would represent good things in the future, and blue would represent bad things in the future. This time around, a very different picture took place. There were almost no blue pins to be found. People, despite having just shown how much blue and yellow there was in the past, overwhelming didn't predict anything bad happening in the future.

We are very, very, very bad at predicting the future.

Here is a list of things that can go wrong - and we can never truly be prepared for because they are not things we can know are coming until they have already happened:

- Sickness in the family
- You lose your job
- Your car breaks down
- Your apartment floods and you need to find a new   place to live
- You lose your job and your car breaks down
- Your dog gets sick
- You hit someone in a fury of rage in the local Starbucks and now have to pay a huge fine
- You finally return your library books after 10 years and have to pay another huge fine
- You run out of graduation gift money and have to start paying for things yourself
- Your break both your legs

And that's just what I was able to think up on a Monday night with YouTube playing in the background.

So yes, we have saved for the future. We have realized that we may be spending too much money on Starbucks and booze (and have rationalized that we should keep at least one of those things in our lives, we're not nuns). But we must do more than just realize that we don't have to spend so much - we must build a small emergency fund.

We cannot invest unless we have money. We do not have money if we do not start saving for 1) our future and 2) our future unknown problems.

Most experts believe you should have enough money in your emergency fund to cover at least 3 to 6 months' worth of living expenses. This should include housing needs, food, health care, utilities, transportation, insurance, you name it. I also like to think "What if my car broke down right now? Could I afford to fix it? What if my car broke down and my heating broke in winter? Could I fix both?" The emergency fund to me is more than just what if I lose my job - it's what if something goes run that I have no right being prepared for?

You don't need to include expenses for anything you'd cut from your budget in the event of a job loss or major catastrophe. This means anything like going out to the movies, vacations, that new iPhone, etc.
What I want to drive home most though is that you should start saving. What I've talked about above is probably daunting. All these potential problems! I'm not trying to scare you (ok maybe I am, just a little). But when people see all this pretend money going out the door, they clam up and get worried. I'm going to steal from a magnificent book right now:

DON'T PANIC

Something is better than nothing. Don't think you can save enough? Don't panic. Start by putting away a little at a time. Little by little a little becomes a lot. A pile of sand is just a bunch of tiny rocks piled up (man I am deep).

The important thing is that you've started saving something.

For instance, let's say you set aside $25 a week in an emergency fund. At the end of 2 years, you could have $2,600 saved.
Increase that amount to $50 a week and your savings could grow to $5,200. Obviously the more you save, the more you'll get.

One last thing - don't invest this money. The point of these funds is simply to exist. If you invest it, you introduce the risk of losing it all. This money is a safety net, and so, it must be safe.

Chapter 2:
Investing

Or: Tell me that thing rich people do that turns their money into more money

The Key Points
1. Use a Target Date Fund if you have no idea what you are doing
2. Use an index fund
3. Active managers don't do better than index funds, and cost a lot of money
4. Diversify your investments (be invested in more than one thing)
5. DON'T PANIC if the market is doing badly
6. Check in on your portfolio every once in a while - you've got 40+ years for things to work out

The Basics

At this point, we've covered that it's crucial to save. We get it, Mike! Teach me how to invest! Teach me what investing even is! I'm going to make a few assumptions:

- You have a job and are willing to set aside some money
  and/or
- Your company has a 401(k) or similar investment option

If you don't have a 401(k) but still want to invest I suggest opening up a brokerage account at one of the cheap online choices like eTrade, Schwab, or use the app Robinhood (free trading at this one). Also, if you have a question about any of the words I'm using, the 4th chapter is a bunch of definitions. Don't know what a 401(k) is? Find the answer there. Don't know what the S&P 500 is? Find the answer there. You have absolutely no clue what a Roth IRA is? Find the answer there.

Most companies offer some sort of retirement plan. It is imperative you take advantage of this. It's so important that most companies auto-enroll you without you even realizing it, diverting on average 3% of your pay to a retirement plan.

Most American's only have $38,000 saved by the time they are set to retire. That is, of course, not enough. But you're smart; you bought this book! So yes, you'll save for retirement.

First things first: put as much as possible into your retirement account, especially if your company offers a "match".

Here's an example:

Joe saves 6% of his salary in his 401(k). His company has a policy that they will match 100% of his contributions up to 6% of his total salary. Joe makes $100,000 a year. This means he contributes $6000 a year to his 401(k), and his company adds $6000! He has already gotten a return of 100% on his money! And best of all, all this money is tax-free!

That means he doesn't have to pay any taxes on that $12,000 or any future earnings on his money. So all his future earnings won't be taxed, and the government will only tax him on $94,000 of his $100,000 (if he doesn't do anything else to lower his taxes).

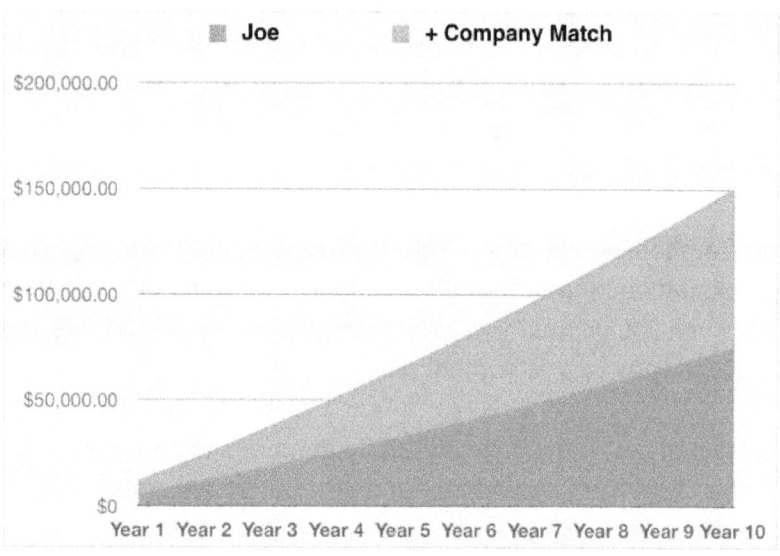

The more money put into an investment in the beginning, the more it will grow. The below chart highlights contributions of Joe's investment alone, and with company match, with an interest rate of 5% a year:

Wow, so far Joe is doing pretty well. But all he did was put his money into a 401(k) account. In what should he invest? What should you invest in?

Most Common Options

There are two options most companies offer:
- Target Date Funds
- A bunch of random funds

Most people are auto-enrolled into a Target Date Fund (TDF, from here on). So what does that mean? TDFs are funds that do all the heavy lifting for you. They base your investment universe on your age. So if you're 25 and the year is currently 2015, your TDF is TRD-2060. This means that the fund is betting that you're going to retire in 2060.

If you're 25, the fund is going to give you mostly equities (stocks, like Apple). The TDF will say "you're young, so we're going to give you 90% stocks, and 10% in bonds." As you get older, say 45, the TDF will automatically change the amount of stocks versus bonds.

The older you get, the less risky you should be. Stocks are riskier than bonds. So at the age of 45, the TDF will automatically move to a mix of 50% stocks and 50% bonds (as an example). The thing you have to know is this isn't always cheap. Because you're making someone else do all the work they are going to charge you for it. But at the end of it, you will probably have had a pretty well-managed investment portfolio without having to think about it.

TL;DR: *Target Date Funds make all the investment decisions for you, but they may cost you a lot more than managing funds yourself.*

If that sounds good to you, congrats! You can stop reading and watch cat videos on the internet.

Doing It Yourself

But maybe you don't want to use a TDF, or you only have a brokerage account and want to invest everything your way. Here are a few guidelines.

- If you're young, stay mostly in stocks
- And by stocks, I mean in index funds (index funds are explained below)
- As you get older, move more and more into fixed income
- A good rule of thumb is the rule of 100:
- Take 100, less your age, and that is how much you should be in stocks
- If you are 30, you portfolio should be roughly 70% in stocks
- A few things to stay away from are active management and picking individual stocks.
-

Active management is too expensive at your level of income. While it can be argued that some managers do have a track record that supports that they beat benchmarks, almost all active managers have just as many good years as bad years, and the benchmark wins. So all in all, it's not worth the cost.

Above is what you would get by investing $100 in the most commonly used investment. It is the S&P 500 index, what most people mean when they talk about the "stock market". An active manager, on average, does not beat the market. (Historically speaking, many do *worse* than the market). But we are going to pretend that an active manager is doing just as well as the S&P 500.

The problem is that an index fund costs next to nothing, but an active manager will charge you for their "expertise". The average cost as of 2015 was .8%. That doesn't sound like a lot, but if you invested in 1985, and took out your money in 2015...the difference can add up.

Blue line is using the S&P 500 index, green line is using an active manager.

Picking Stocks

Picking individual stocks can also be a bad idea. While some people can do it, and I do make a few picks every once in awhile, individual stock picking can lead many people to buy when things are expensive and selling when things get cheap, meaning they mostly make bad decisions and lose money.

"Darn it Mike! What should I be doing with my money then!?" You ask.

Buy index funds. An index fund is a basket of stocks that is very cheap to own. You gain whatever the stock market gains, and for almost no cost. So if the S&P 500 (what most people refer to as the U.S. stock market) goes up 5% in a year, you go up 5% in a year.

What you also get from an index fund is cheap diversification. Diversification is spreading your money out on a bunch of different bets (buying 500 companies with the S&P 500 index for $100) instead of only being able to buy one share of one company for $100.

Speaking of diversification, there's something else you should do to be best diversified - buy more than one index fund. You should try to capture different parts of the stock market, and of the world. Below is how I would structure my portfolio at 25:

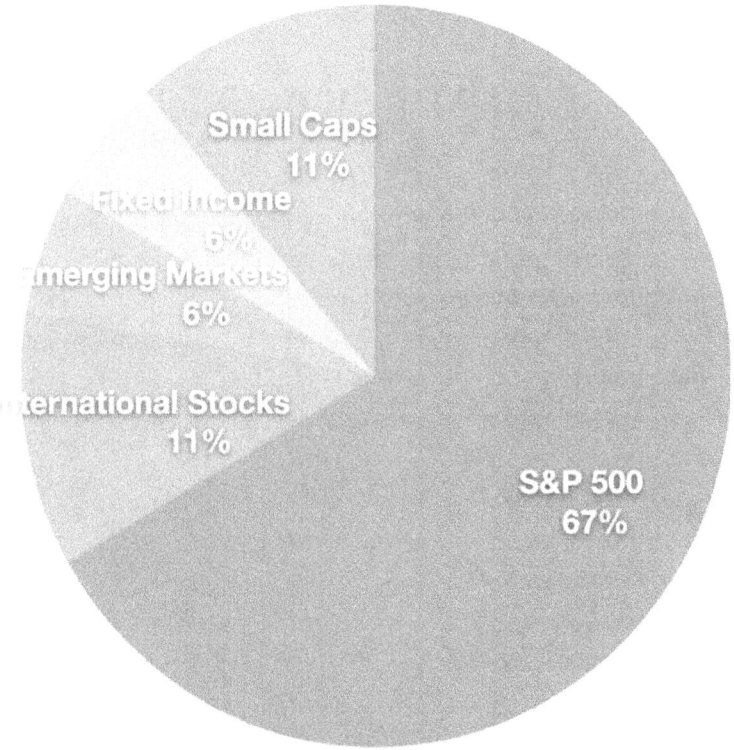

You can get access to everything above using just five funds (1 fund for each section above). Again, a comprehensive list of what anything above (like Emerging Markets) is is in the next chapter. I added a little bit more fixed income to the above example than the "100 Rule" says because I'm pretty conservative in my investments.

But back to diversification: If I had wanted to get a good diversification like the above buying individual stocks I would have to buy a ton of different shares of stocks, thousands, and thousands. That would cost a lot of money, and take a lot of time. By purchasing index funds, I save time and money. Two things of which I am a big fan.

Once you've bought your initial portfolio I need you to do one thing:

DON'T LOOK AT IT

Seriously. Please. Don't look at your investment portfolio for a long time. A couple of months, a year even. I move money around maybe once a year at most. As I get older each year I take more money out of the riskier investments and put a little more into the less-risky assets.
Our five assets listed above are listed as least risky to most risky:

- Fixed Income
- S&P 500
- International
- Small Cap
- Emerging Markets

So each year I might take a little more out of emerging markets and small cap, and move more into the S&P 500 or Fixed Income as an example. Honestly, I might not even change the amount I have invested in Emerging Markets for instance for years and years because I know that investing takes time, and you can't judge an investment day by day, month by month, or even after a year or so.

Every person who panics on a daily basis about their portfolio buys and sells at all the wrong times because they keep checking and get worried or excited at every little up and down movement in their portfolio. And when things go wrong in the world? Like the financial crisis? That's when the most people panic and sell - the exact time you should hold onto what you have.

If people sold during the financial crisis and bought back their stocks a year later, they lost a ton of money. The people who just stayed put got some of the best returns of their life, just by waiting (or forgetting to check their portfolio).

If you ever forget, I've made the following page just for you. If something big is happening in the world, and you get worried about your money and fear takes hold and you think it's time to pull out because the world is ending…

DON'T PANIC

So to review:

- Buy index funds
- Don't use active management
- The younger you are, the more you should be in stocks
- Use the Rule of 100 is you are unsure how much to be in stocks
- You should diversify your holdings in a few different funds and index types
- Things go up and down in the market all the time, don't panic
- For the love of god don't check your portfolio every day.

Chapter 3:
Debt (Is Evil Spelled Incorrectly)

Or: How to ruin your life

The Key points
1. **Debt can be useful sometimes, like to buy a house**
2. **Credit cards are too easy too use**
3. **Don't use debt for everything**
4. **You will be told to take on lots of debt by very smart people, they are wrong**

One last thing. Sit down, won't you? I want to give you the talk. What? No not that talk. I want to talk to you about debt. There are going to be a lot of people trying to make you take on debt in the next few years. Friends, family, banks, credit card companies...a lot of people. Don't listen to them.

You don't need debt. You just don't. (Ok, it can be helpful, but for the most part you should stay away from it. I'm trying to make a point here).

So what is debt, really? Debt is telling someone that you'll pay them later, and paying extra because you're putting off paying. So if you buy a $10 meal and put it on your credit card this is what happens: The credit card company pays the restaurant, and now you owe the credit card company $10. But because they fronted money on your behalf, they're going to charge you $1. So now you really paid $11 for that meal. This is not ideal. Debt, credit cards, doesn't need to be used for everything.

Debt is a way to buy something that costs a lot, but pay for it a little at a time. That doesn't sound so bad, does it? The problem starts when you start using debt for everything. Groceries, that cool drone on Amazon, socks. Or it starts when you see something you need, like a car or a house, and see that someone is willing to loan you even more than you need. You could get that nicer car! That bigger house! Someone offering you a loan do not care about that, they care that they can have you on the hook for even more debt.

Debt is a drug. It is so easy to use, and so hard to get away from.

Here's the real way to use it:

Don't get a credit card for a long time. As long as you can. Using one does help you get a credit score, however, so if you do get one use it sparingly. Use it once a month for a small purchase and pay it off as soon as possible. Keep doing this for as long as you can, until you get a better credit card with a lower interest rate. The more credit you use, the worse you look. So if the card has a limit of $500, and you always use $500 a month, you look worse than the person who only uses $100 of credit a month.

The truth is if you can't afford it without using debt, you probably shouldn't be getting it. A car, sure. A house, maybe (depending on your living situation). You should plan out how much you can pay each month, and only go into debt for as much as you can realistically afford. Like I said above, someone will usually give you a larger loan. "Just enough rope to hang yourself," as my Grandpa would say.

Chapter 4: Definitions

Or: All those words people keep throwing around

Net Worth:
How much you are worth. If you have no debt, and own a car worth $12,000 and have savings of $2000, your Net Worth is $14,000. If you also have debt (like student loans) of $50,000, your Net Worth is negative $36,000

Investing:
Putting money into a riskier asset than cash (aka your savings account) in the hope that you will have more money later on by taking on risk.

A retirement account:
An account, usually that has incentives like the government not taxing you on any money you put into this account, that you would use the save money for later on in your life when you are retired. Generally speaking, this is where you will do most of your investing.

401(k):
The most common type of retirement account. This is offered by most private-sector (non-government) jobs. Any money you put into this account won't be taxed by the government.

403(b):
Like a 401(k), but for government workers (teachers, mailmen, etc)

Index fund:

A type of investment that covers a large area of the investment universe. So if you by the S&P 500 index fund, you're buying an index that performs the same as the S&P 500. An index fund is good for an everyday investor because you get exposure to a ton of stocks in one fell swoop and it costs very little

Stocks:

A stock represents ownership in a company. So if there are 100 shares of stock for the company Apple, and you buy 1 stock of Apple, you own 1% of Apple. This means you have 1% of the voting rights in the company. Also, if Apple is worth $100, your share is worth $1. If Apple is worth $200 a year from now, your share is worth $2. Stock is generally riskier than bonds, because in the event a business goes bankrupt, bondholders are paid first. Therefore, stockholders usually ask for higher returns on their investment than bondholders.

Equities:

Another word for stocks

Bonds:

A form of debt. If Apple sells you a bond worth $100, and you pay them $99 now, they are in debt to you for $100. If the timeframe is a year, that means you will make $1 in a year. Bonds are less risky than stocks because they are legally responsible for giving you money before stockholders. Therefore because bondholders are more likely to get a gain on their investment, they are willing to have a lower return.

Fixed Income:

Another word for bonds

The S&P 500:

This is an index of the 500 largest public companies in the United States. This is the most commonly used index in America, and what most people mean when they are talking about "how the stock market did today".

Small Cap Stocks:

Companies that are worth around $300 million to $2 billion. These companies are inherently more risky to invest in, but also have the highest growth rates. So if you want to get a little riskier in your stock holdings, here's where you might go.

Mid Cap Stocks:

A company worth between $2 billion and $10 billion. These are, not surprisingly, in between small and large cap companies. They are mid-risk and mid-returns generally.

Large Cap Stocks:

Companies worth $10 billion or more. These are the most stable companies that you can buy (generally speaking, there's always that one guy in the group who is a little unstable). These are the companies you are probably most familiar with - Apple, Google, Bank of America. These companies have generally lower returns than small caps, but are more reliable and less risky. These are what I invest in most of the time.

Emerging Markets:

This refers to a geographic region of the world (usually involving countries like Vietnam, South Africa, etc). They are kind of like the small cap stocks definition - more risky and unstable, but also can offer very high returns for someone willing to take that risk.

International:
A geographic region that, as an American Investor, usually means Europe, Japan, and a few other countries in that area.

Company Match:
The % a company will contribute to your retirement account directly related to how much you contribute. So if you contribute $100 a year, and you make $1000 a year, your contribution rate is 10%. If the company also contribute $50, that means they have a 100% match up to 5% of your salary.

IRA:
An Individual Retirement Account. You can open this on your own. A company doesn't sponsor this like a 401(k).

An annuity:
If you are young and offered one of these, run away from this person very fast. An annuity is giving someone lots of money now so they can give it back to you later in life in little chunks at a time.

A financial advisor:
Someone who will help you manage your investments, for a fee. Generally speaking there are three ways they can be paid: hourly, fee-based, or on commission. If you are speaking to a financial advisor, ask them how they are compensated first. Commission means they generally have an incentive to sell you very specific things, regardless of what is best for you. I would personally go with someone on a fee or hourly basis. There are good and bad financial advisors, just like in every other field.

Passive Investing:
Investing in an index fund, that tracks a broad market. This costs very little and is a good way to invest without too much work.

Active Investing:

Someone picking very specific stocks to buy or sell, in an attempt to "beat the market". If you are thinking about using an active fund, know that most active investors don't beat the market in the long run, and after the fees they charge you you may be doing even worse than an index fund anyways.

Dividends:

A cash payment a company pays to stockholders, usually every 3 months. Not every company does this, and the amount paid varies.

Interest Rates:

The amount you pay someone to borrow money (mortgage), or that they pay you to borrow your money (savings account)

Diversification:

Being in a lot of different investments at the same time. Diversification is important. This way you don't put all your money into one company that might seem to be doing really well, let's say Enron, that ends up totally corrupt and terrible and all your money goes away.

Growth Stocks/Growth Investing:

Investing in companies that are inherently more risky but have larger return potentials in their future (think Facebook when it was first starting)

Value Stocks/Value Investing:

Investing in companies with really stable revenue streams and are already probably somewhat established (think Apple) that also seem to be kind of cheap

P/E Ratio:
Price over earnings. That means how much a stock cost versus earnings. So if a stock costs $160, and the earnings were $10 for that share, the P/E is 16. Most companies have a P/E ratio of around 16

Yield:
How much you will get on your investment in a bond. If you bought a bond for $100, and you will get $105 in a year, your yield is 5%

Money Market:
Kind of like a checking account, a super safe investment to store your cash in your retirement account

Stable Value Fund:
Like a money market, with slightly higher interest rate. Sometimes there are restrictions in putting in/taking out money really fast

Company Stock:
Your company's stock (if it has any public stock). A lot of public companies will reward higher-level employees with company stock as a reward. This also means that the person's wealth is now tied to how well the company does, incentivizing them to work harder. Some people have close to 25% of their investments in company stock. Please don't be like that person. There are too many stories of people having even 90% of their wealth in company stock, and then the company goes bankrupt and lives are ruined. Not great.

Thanks for reading!